Living in a Biome

Life in a Stream

by Carol K. Lindeen

Consulting Editor: Gail Saunders-Smith, Ph.D.
Consultant: Sandra Mather, Professor Emerita
Department of Geology and Astronomy, West Chester University
West Chester, Pennsylvania

Mankato, Minnesota

Pebble Plus is published by Capstone Press
151 Good Counsel Drive, P.O. Box 669, Mankato, Minnesota 56002
http://www.capstonepress.com

1 2 3 4 5 6 08 07 06 05 04 03

Library of Congress Cataloging-in-Publication Data
Lindeen, Carol K., 1976–
    Life in a stream / by Carol K. Lindeen.
    p. cm.—(Pebble plus: Living in a biome)
    Summary: Simple text and photographs introduce the stream biome, including
the environment, plants, and animals.
    Includes bibliographical references (p. 23) and index.
    ISBN 0-7368-3404-4 (softcover) ISBN 0-7368-2103-1 (hardcover)
    1. Stream animals—Juvenile literature. 2. Stream plants—Juvenile literature.
[1. Stream animals. 2. Stream plants.] I. Title. II. Series.
QH97 .L56 2004
578.764—dc21   2002155686

Editorial Credits
Martha E. H. Rustad, editor; Kia Adams, designer and illustrator; Juliette Peters, cover production designer; Kelly Garvin, photo researcher;
  Eric Kudalis, product planning editor

Photo Credits
Ann & Rob Simpson, 16–17
Corbis, 1
Digital Vision, cover
James P. Rowan, 18–19
Minden Pictures/Michael Quinton, 8–9
Robert McCaw, 10–11, 12–13
Tom Stack & Associates/Brian Parker, 4–5; Peter Mead, 6–7, 14–15; Thomas Kitchin, 20–21

Note to Parents and Teachers

The Living in a Biome series supports national science standards related to life science. This book describes and illustrates animal and plant life in streams. The photographs support early readers in understanding the text. This book also introduces early readers to subject-specific vocabulary words, which are defined in the Glossary section. Early readers may need assistance to read some words and to use the Table of Contents, Glossary, Read More, Internet Sites, and Index/Word List sections of the book.

Word Count: 109
Early-Intervention Level: 12

Table of Contents

What Are Streams?

A stream is a long body
of flowing water. Streams
are smaller than rivers.

Streams flow through cold
places and warm places.
Streams often flow into
rivers or lakes.

Stream Animals

Fish swim in streams. Fish
eat insects, other small
animals, and plants.

Insects live near streams.

Water striders can walk

on the water.

Bears catch and eat fish
from streams. Bears live in
the woods near streams.

Stream Plants

Plants grow near streams.

Some plants grow under

the water.

Trees grow along the shores
of streams.

Moss often grows on rocks,
trees, and the wet shore.

Living Together

Animals find food in streams.
Stream water helps plants
grow. Streams are full
of life.

Glossary

flow—to move along smoothly; water in a stream flows in one direction.

insect—a small animal with a hard outer shell, three body sections, six legs, and two antennas; most insects have two or four wings.

lake—a large body of water with land on all sides; most lakes are freshwater lakes.

moss—a soft, short plant with no roots; moss grows on damp soil, rocks, and tree trunks.

river—a large body of flowing water

shore—the land along the edge of a body of water

woods—a large area covered with trees and plants; forests are sometimes called woods.

Read More

Baldwin, Carol. *Living by a River.* Living Habitats. Chicago: Heinemann Library, 2003.

Oxlade, Chris. *Rivers and Lakes.* Science Files—Earth. Milwaukee: Gareth Stevens, 2003.

Pascoe, Elaine. *The Ecosystem of a Stream.* Library of Small Ecosystems. New York: PowerKids Press, 2003.

Internet Sites

Do you want to find out more about streams?
Let FactHound, our fact-finding hound dog, do the research for you.

Here's how:

1) Visit *http://www.facthound.com*

2) Type in the **Book ID** number: **0736821031**

3) Click on **FETCH IT**.

FactHound will fetch Internet sites picked by our editors just for you!

Index/Word List